INGRI & EDGAR PARIN D'AULAIRE

BENJAMIN FRANKLIN

ISBN: 0-385-07219-8

DOUBLEDAY & COMPANY, INC., GARDEN CITY, NEW YORK

15 14 13

At the time when the King of England ruled over the American colonies there stood a small house on Milk Street in Boston.

In this house there lived a candlemaker whose name was Josiah Franklin. He was a good and pious man, and the Lord had given him a virtuous wife and a blessing of seventeen children, all counted.

Three times each Sunday he led all his children to church and he taught them to be honest and hard-working and satisfied with little.

"He who knows his trade does not have to stand except for kings," said Josiah Franklin. He looked proudly at his ten husky sons and hoped that someday they would all be good tradesmen.

One Today is Worth

Two Tomorrows

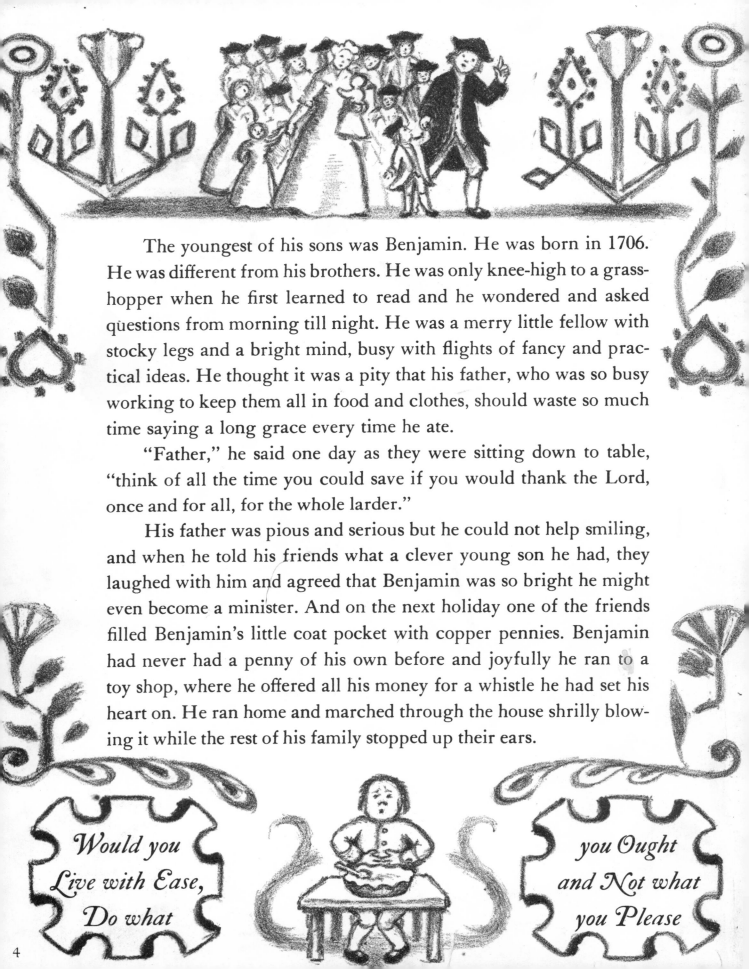

The youngest of his sons was Benjamin. He was born in 1706. He was different from his brothers. He was only knee-high to a grasshopper when he first learned to read and he wondered and asked questions from morning till night. He was a merry little fellow with stocky legs and a bright mind, busy with flights of fancy and practical ideas. He thought it was a pity that his father, who was so busy working to keep them all in food and clothes, should waste so much time saying a long grace every time he ate.

"Father," he said one day as they were sitting down to table, "think of all the time you could save if you would thank the Lord, once and for all, for the whole larder."

His father was pious and serious but he could not help smiling, and when he told his friends what a clever young son he had, they laughed with him and agreed that Benjamin was so bright he might even become a minister. And on the next holiday one of the friends filled Benjamin's little coat pocket with copper pennies. Benjamin had never had a penny of his own before and joyfully he ran to a toy shop, where he offered all his money for a whistle he had set his heart on. He ran home and marched through the house shrilly blowing it while the rest of his family stopped up their ears.

Would you Live with Ease, Do what

you Ought and Not what you Please

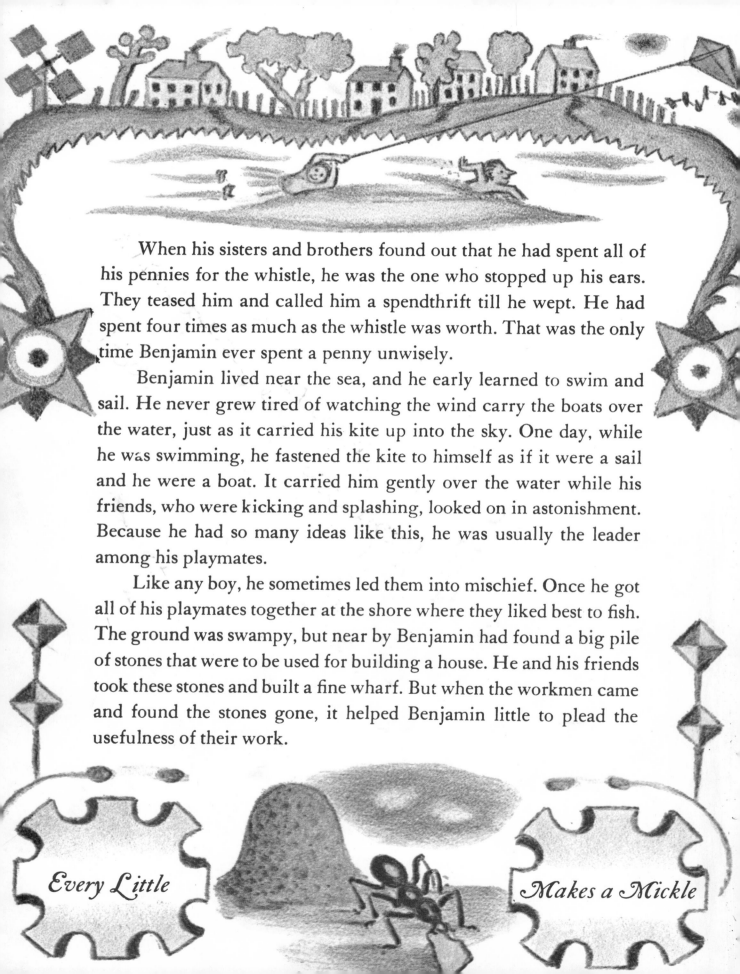

When his sisters and brothers found out that he had spent all of his pennies for the whistle, he was the one who stopped up his ears. They teased him and called him a spendthrift till he wept. He had spent four times as much as the whistle was worth. That was the only time Benjamin ever spent a penny unwisely.

Benjamin lived near the sea, and he early learned to swim and sail. He never grew tired of watching the wind carry the boats over the water, just as it carried his kite up into the sky. One day, while he was swimming, he fastened the kite to himself as if it were a sail and he were a boat. It carried him gently over the water while his friends, who were kicking and splashing, looked on in astonishment. Because he had so many ideas like this, he was usually the leader among his playmates.

Like any boy, he sometimes led them into mischief. Once he got all of his playmates together at the shore where they liked best to fish. The ground was swampy, but near by Benjamin had found a big pile of stones that were to be used for building a house. He and his friends took these stones and built a fine wharf. But when the workmen came and found the stones gone, it helped Benjamin little to plead the usefulness of their work.

Every Little

Makes a Mickle

After he had been soundly spanked by his father, Benjamin was convinced that nothing is useful that is not honest.

When Benjamin was eight years old, his father sent him to grammar school. He rose to the head of his class in reading and writing, and he read every book he could lay his hands upon. But he was poor in arithmetic. His father began to think that perhaps Benjamin should be a tradesman like his brothers. So, when Benjamin was ten years old, he was taken out of school to learn his father's trade of candlemaking.

Benjamin hated dipping candles and cutting wicks the whole day long. He read and he dreamed. More and more he dreamed about ships and voyages to faraway ports. His father began to fear that his son might become a sailor and be lost at sea. Hoping to find Benjamin a trade that he would really like, he took him to call on joiners and braziers and cutlers and bricklayers in their workshops. Benjamin learned much about these trades but he did not want to follow any of them. At last his worried father persuaded him that, since he was so fond of books, he should become a printer's apprentice. Then he could look at the printed word all day long.

His older brother James had a printing shop and, when Benja-

At the Working Man's House

Hunger looks in but Dares not Enter

min was twelve, he moved from his father's house and bound himself to be his brother's apprentice for nine years. In return, James was to teach him to print and to give him his board and clothes.

James was a strict master. When his young brother answered back with his quick wit and ready tongue, he boxed his ears severely. Benjamin had to sweep the floor, wash the type, and do all the dirty work while he watched his brother and his helpers print pamphlets and books. By and by James taught him to set type and print.

Benjamin was a hard-working boy and he learned fast. In a few years he was his brother's best worker. He would have liked life in the printing shop very much if he had had more time to read all the books around him. One day he had one of his practical ideas. He asked his brother to give him half of the money he paid for Benjamin's board so he could get his own meals and eat them in the shop when the others went out. James did not mind. He saved money. And Benjamin was happy. Now he had time to read books in peace while he ate his gruel and munched an apple. He did not care much what he ate as long as it was cheap and wholesome. He soon found that he could save half of the money his brother gave him for food. With that he bought books.

Early to Bed and Early to Rise, Makes

a Man Healthy, Wealthy, and Wise

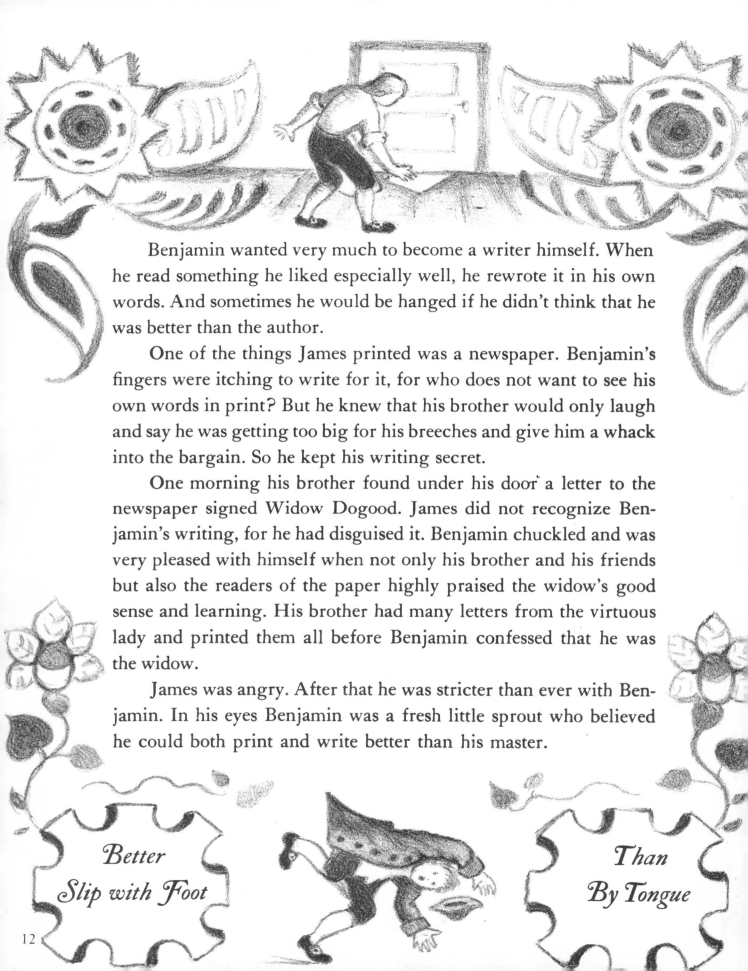

Benjamin wanted very much to become a writer himself. When he read something he liked especially well, he rewrote it in his own words. And sometimes he would be hanged if he didn't think that he was better than the author.

One of the things James printed was a newspaper. Benjamin's fingers were itching to write for it, for who does not want to see his own words in print? But he knew that his brother would only laugh and say he was getting too big for his breeches and give him a whack into the bargain. So he kept his writing secret.

One morning his brother found under his door a letter to the newspaper signed Widow Dogood. James did not recognize Benjamin's writing, for he had disguised it. Benjamin chuckled and was very pleased with himself when not only his brother and his friends but also the readers of the paper highly praised the widow's good sense and learning. His brother had many letters from the virtuous lady and printed them all before Benjamin confessed that he was the widow.

James was angry. After that he was stricter than ever with Benjamin. In his eyes Benjamin was a fresh little sprout who believed he could both print and write better than his master.

Better Slip with Foot

Than By Tongue

Benjamin thought he was now too big to be thrashed by his brother. He had been his apprentice for five years and had become a very good printer. Yes, he had even run the printing shop alone while his brother was away. He asked his brother please to let him go so that he could find work for himself elsewhere. But James said no, he must stay till his nine years were up.

Then Benjamin made up his mind to run away. He knew it was wrong but he could no longer stand his brother's harsh treatment. He sold some of his cherished books to get a little money, and late one night he secretly boarded a ship bound for New York. He stood at the rail watching his native town vanish into the night. He felt small and lonesome. His parents would be sad and his brother would be angry. He was only seventeen and he did not know a soul in New York who might help him.

The winds were fair, but even so the trip to New York took three days. During a lull the sailors fished and made a big haul of cod. They invited Benjamin to eat with them, but Benjamin said no, thank you, he ate neither flesh nor fish, for he had read in a book that it was murder to kill and eat creatures that had done him no harm. But he loved codfish and, when the fish was cooking and the good smells

He that Doth What He Should Not,

Shall Feel What He Would Not

14

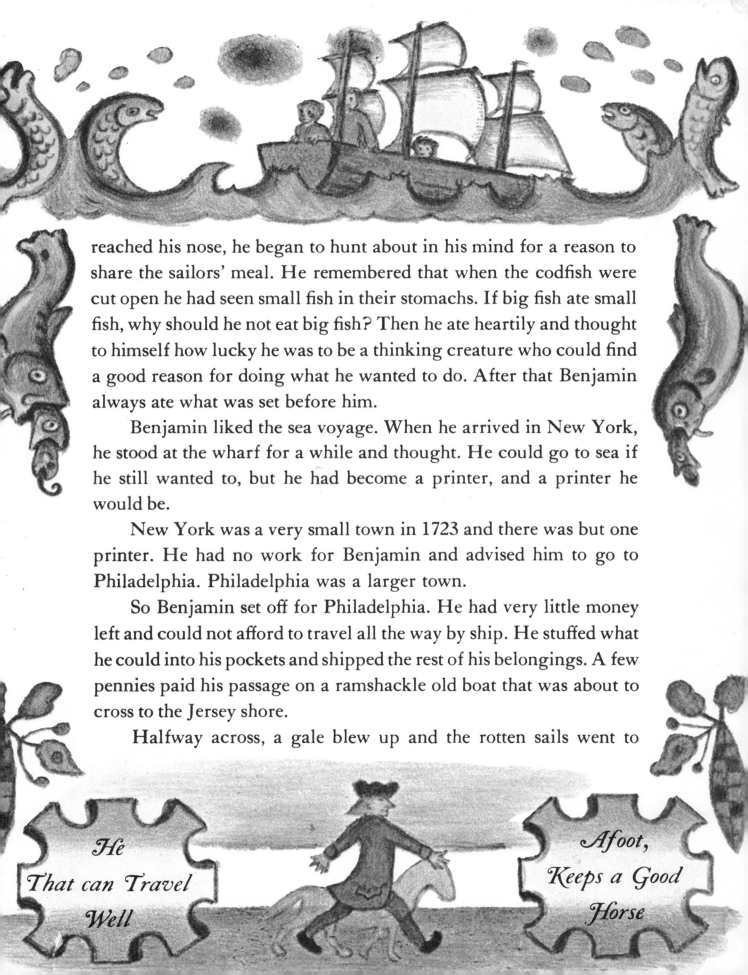

reached his nose, he began to hunt about in his mind for a reason to share the sailors' meal. He remembered that when the codfish were cut open he had seen small fish in their stomachs. If big fish ate small fish, why should he not eat big fish? Then he ate heartily and thought to himself how lucky he was to be a thinking creature who could find a good reason for doing what he wanted to do. After that Benjamin always ate what was set before him.

Benjamin liked the sea voyage. When he arrived in New York, he stood at the wharf for a while and thought. He could go to sea if he still wanted to, but he had become a printer, and a printer he would be.

New York was a very small town in 1723 and there was but one printer. He had no work for Benjamin and advised him to go to Philadelphia. Philadelphia was a larger town.

So Benjamin set off for Philadelphia. He had very little money left and could not afford to travel all the way by ship. He stuffed what he could into his pockets and shipped the rest of his belongings. A few pennies paid his passage on a ramshackle old boat that was about to cross to the Jersey shore.

Halfway across, a gale blew up and the rotten sails went to

He That can Travel Well

Afoot, Keeps a Good Horse

pieces. In the storm a Dutchman fell overboard. Benjamin quickly grabbed him by the hair and pulled him back into the boat. The dripping Dutchman pulled a book out of his pocket and asked Benjamin to dry it for him. It was the most beautiful book Benjamin had ever seen. It had been printed in Europe with fine type and many pictures. That was the kind of book he would like to print.

He had plenty of time to enjoy the book, for the boat pitched and tossed in the bay of New York for thirty hours. At last the crew managed to bring her to port on the Jersey shore and, cold and wet, Benjamin started to walk. It was a long way on foot, for it is a hundred miles from New York to Philadelphia.

For days he trudged through ruts and mud, in rain and storm, and he began to be sorry he had ever run away. When he reached the Delaware River, he was lucky. A small boat came sailing downstream and the crew took him on board. But soon the wind died down. Benjamin had to help row the boat till his hands were covered with blisters. He looked so bedraggled and forlorn, it was a wonder he was not sent home as a runaway bound boy.

That is the way he arrived in Philadelphia early on a Sunday morning. People in their Sunday-go-to-meeting clothes were walking

Light Purse,

Heavy Heart

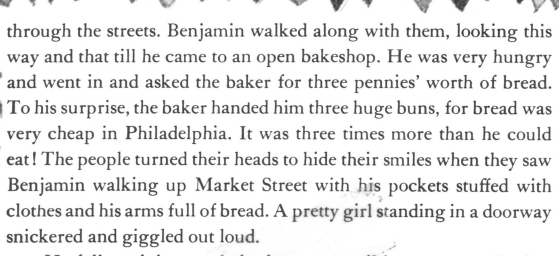

through the streets. Benjamin walked along with them, looking this way and that till he came to an open bakeshop. He was very hungry and went in and asked the baker for three pennies' worth of bread. To his surprise, the baker handed him three huge buns, for bread was very cheap in Philadelphia. It was three times more than he could eat! The people turned their heads to hide their smiles when they saw Benjamin walking up Market Street with his pockets stuffed with clothes and his arms full of bread. A pretty girl standing in a doorway snickered and giggled out loud.

He followed the people in the street until he came to a Quaker meetinghouse, which he entered. He was so exhausted that he fell asleep the moment he sat down. He had come to the city of brotherly love, so nobody woke him till the meeting was over. Then a kind Quaker showed him to an inn where he could rest and eat.

Scrubbed and refreshed, Benjamin went out the next morning, and soon he found work as a printer's helper. Nobody laughed at his looks any longer, but everybody laughed at his jokes. It was not long before the people in Philadelphia were telling one another how lucky it was that such a good printer and fine young fellow had settled in their town. Many of them made friends with him. The governor of

An Empty Bag

Can Not Stand Upright

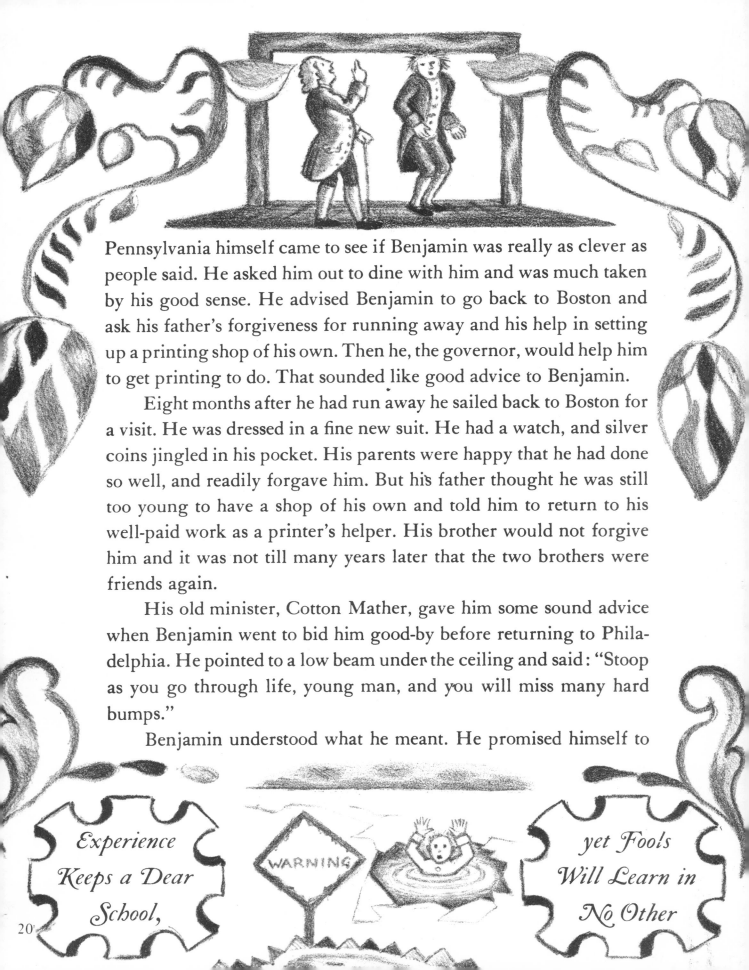

Pennsylvania himself came to see if Benjamin was really as clever as people said. He asked him out to dine with him and was much taken by his good sense. He advised Benjamin to go back to Boston and ask his father's forgiveness for running away and his help in setting up a printing shop of his own. Then he, the governor, would help him to get printing to do. That sounded like good advice to Benjamin.

Eight months after he had run away he sailed back to Boston for a visit. He was dressed in a fine new suit. He had a watch, and silver coins jingled in his pocket. His parents were happy that he had done so well, and readily forgave him. But his father thought he was still too young to have a shop of his own and told him to return to his well-paid work as a printer's helper. His brother would not forgive him and it was not till many years later that the two brothers were friends again.

His old minister, Cotton Mather, gave him some sound advice when Benjamin went to bid him good-by before returning to Philadelphia. He pointed to a low beam under the ceiling and said: "Stoop as you go through life, young man, and you will miss many hard bumps."

Benjamin understood what he meant. He promised himself to

Experience Keeps a Dear School,

WARNING

yet Fools Will Learn in No Other

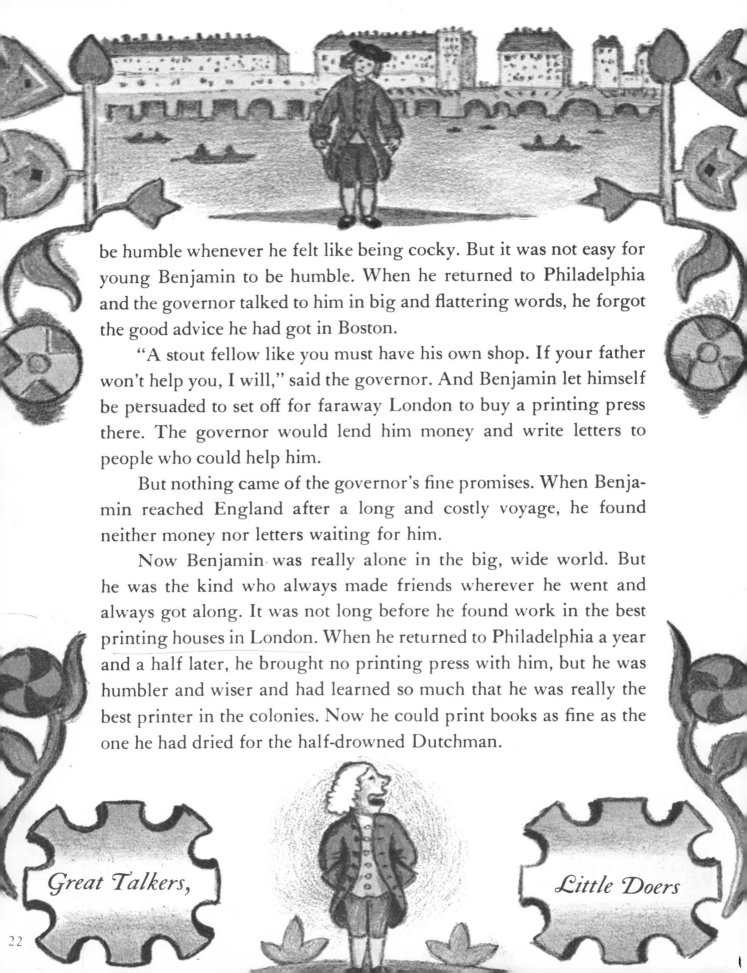

be humble whenever he felt like being cocky. But it was not easy for young Benjamin to be humble. When he returned to Philadelphia and the governor talked to him in big and flattering words, he forgot the good advice he had got in Boston.

"A stout fellow like you must have his own shop. If your father won't help you, I will," said the governor. And Benjamin let himself be persuaded to set off for faraway London to buy a printing press there. The governor would lend him money and write letters to people who could help him.

But nothing came of the governor's fine promises. When Benjamin reached England after a long and costly voyage, he found neither money nor letters waiting for him.

Now Benjamin was really alone in the big, wide world. But he was the kind who always made friends wherever he went and always got along. It was not long before he found work in the best printing houses in London. When he returned to Philadelphia a year and a half later, he brought no printing press with him, but he was humbler and wiser and had learned so much that he was really the best printer in the colonies. Now he could print books as fine as the one he had dried for the half-drowned Dutchman.

Great Talkers,

Little Doers

His old master was only too glad to take him back, and it was not long before his faithful friends helped him to get a printing shop of his own. There he worked early and there he worked late, but for his friends he always had time. He lent them his books. He taught them what he had learned. He started a club called the Junto, where young tradesmen could gather and learn from one another.

He was merry and happy and, though he was a master printer now, he did not hold himself too grand for any work. His fellow townsmen saw him pushing his papers through the streets on a wheelbarrow. "He will go far," one neighbor said to the other. "We see him at work when we get up. He is still working when we go to bed."

He saved every penny he made and in this way he could not help but prosper He got more and more printing to do and soon he had a house of his own and helpers and apprentices working for him. He began to look for a thrifty and hard-working wife. And whom should he marry in the end but the girl who had stood in the doorway and laughed when he first came to town! Her name was Deborah Read. She did not care much about reading or writing, but she admired her Benjamin above all and she made him a good wife.

A little House well filled, A little

Wife Well willed, Are Great Riches

She ran his house. She helped him in the shop. She wasted no money on finery, idle servants, or costly food. They lived well and happily together and soon they had a son and daughter of their own. There was much laughter and gaiety in Benjamin's house, for he was a great one for making jokes and witty puns. It was Benjamin Franklin's wit and common sense that first made him famous up and down the coast of America.

He printed books. He printed pamphlets. He printed a newspaper of his own. When he was twenty-six years old, he also began to print his own calendar. He called it *Poor Richard's Almanack*. He pretended it was written by a poor stargazer whose name was Richard Saunders. Poor Richard had a shrew of a wife who was always scolding him for watching the stars, predicting weather and wind, instead of making a livelihood. To satisfy her, he put his observations into a calendar, hoping that many people would buy it. And the spaces between the dates were filled with puns and funny sayings.

While the whole town slept, Benjamin sat at his desk and chuckled to himself as he wrote Poor Richard's proverbs. And from Rhode Island to North Carolina people chuckled with him. Soon

Don't throw Stones at Your Neighbors

If Your Own Windows are Glass

there was hardly a house where his calendar did not hang on the wall. Poor Richard made Benjamin Franklin prosperous.

Still, he and his family lived as simply as ever. Great was his surprise when he came to breakfast one morning to see a silver spoon and a china dish at his place. He thought an earthen dish and pewter spoon were good enough for him. But his wife said that if her neighbors' husbands could have china and silver, so could her husband, who was a greater man than any of them!

Benjamin Franklin was a good citizen. Though he was busy, he always had time to help others. Soon it came to pass that, if anything was to be done for the welfare of the town, people came to ask his advice. He started a library so that everybody who wanted to read could have books. He started a fine school, for he said that he who teaches himself often has a fool for a master. That school became the University of Pennsylvania. He started a night watch for the protection of honest people. He begged money for a hospital for the poor. He organized a fire department so that the whole town would not burn down. That was the first Volunteer Fire Department in the American colonies and Philadelphia became the safest town. As one of the city fathers, Franklin helped to govern the town. He became

Look Ahead or You Will

Find Yourself Behind

postmaster of Philadelphia, and he was so able that he was made postmaster of all the American colonies. He had become well-to-do and respected.

Benjamin Franklin never cared for money for money's sake, but for the leisure it gave him. He bought himself a larger house where he had room for his books and a quiet study and workroom for himself. While his faithful helpers kept his presses running, he spent long hours in his study. There he used his clear head and skilled fingers to work out many small inventions that would make life simpler for him and his fellow citizens.

Benjamin hated waste. One day, looking at his fireplace, he thought how it ate all the wood he fed it and gave back very little heat. He pitied the women who did much of their work at the fireside. The heat shriveled their faces, and the drafts in the cool room behind them made their backs stiff. So he built a little iron stove with an open front that fitted into the fireplace. The stove drew in the cold drafts, heated the air, and sent the warm air into all the corners of the room. The women blessed him. The fame of the Franklin stove spread even to Europe, but his work on electricity was to mean even more to the world.

A Cat in Gloves

Catches No Mice

28

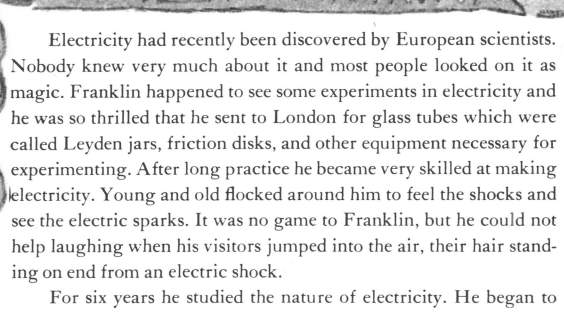

Electricity had recently been discovered by European scientists. Nobody knew very much about it and most people looked on it as magic. Franklin happened to see some experiments in electricity and he was so thrilled that he sent to London for glass tubes which were called Leyden jars, friction disks, and other equipment necessary for experimenting. After long practice he became very skilled at making electricity. Young and old flocked around him to feel the shocks and see the electric sparks. It was no game to Franklin, but he could not help laughing when his visitors jumped into the air, their hair standing on end from an electric shock.

For six years he studied the nature of electricity. He began to wonder if lightning was not caused by electric charges in the clouds. At that time it was believed that thunderstorms were earthquakes in the sky. But it struck Franklin that electric sparks and lightning looked the same, had the same strange smell, and acted in the same way. If lightning was electricity, he could save houses and churches from destruction by putting metal rods on the roofs. The rods would lead the lightning safely away and carry it into the ground. But when Franklin talked about lightning rods, ignorant people protested.

God made earthquakes in the sky to show that He was angry

God Helps Them

That Help Themselves

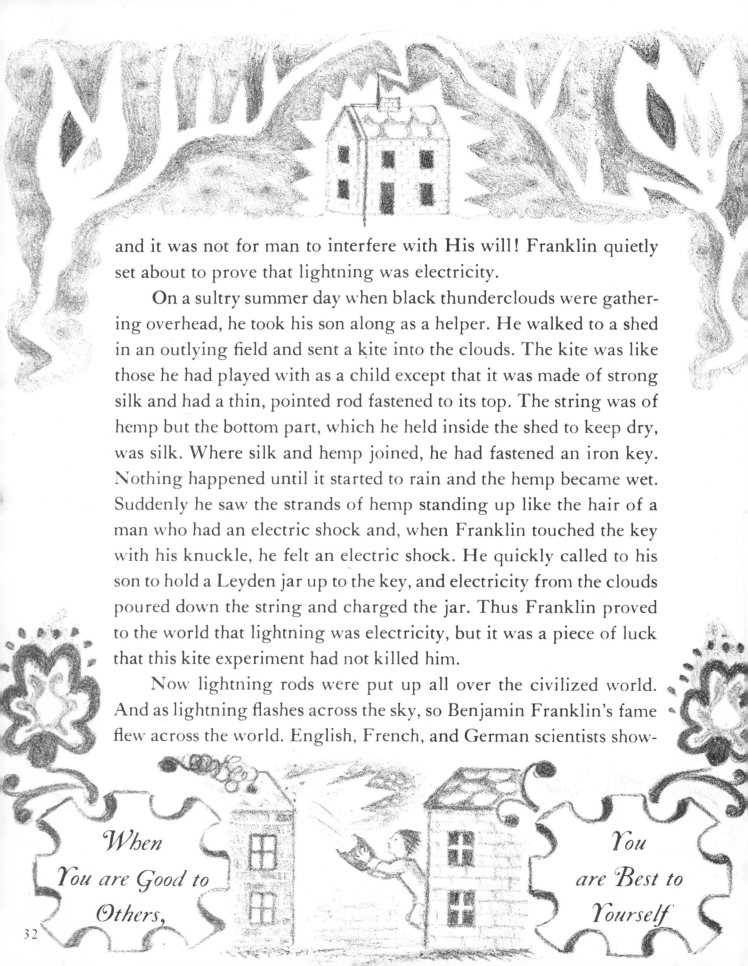

and it was not for man to interfere with His will! Franklin quietly set about to prove that lightning was electricity.

On a sultry summer day when black thunderclouds were gathering overhead, he took his son along as a helper. He walked to a shed in an outlying field and sent a kite into the clouds. The kite was like those he had played with as a child except that it was made of strong silk and had a thin, pointed rod fastened to its top. The string was of hemp but the bottom part, which he held inside the shed to keep dry, was silk. Where silk and hemp joined, he had fastened an iron key. Nothing happened until it started to rain and the hemp became wet. Suddenly he saw the strands of hemp standing up like the hair of a man who had an electric shock and, when Franklin touched the key with his knuckle, he felt an electric shock. He quickly called to his son to hold a Leyden jar up to the key, and electricity from the clouds poured down the string and charged the jar. Thus Franklin proved to the world that lightning was electricity, but it was a piece of luck that this kite experiment had not killed him.

Now lightning rods were put up all over the civilized world. And as lightning flashes across the sky, so Benjamin Franklin's fame flew across the world. English, French, and German scientists show-

When You are Good to Others,

You are Best to Yourself

ered honors upon the inventor, and his fellow Americans were very proud of him. He was made Honorary Doctor of Laws.

Modestly he continued his simple, useful life as a good citizen. And the people of Pennsylvania needed him badly. They asked him to go to England to persuade the King's ministers that Pennsylvania should be allowed to vote her own taxes. For Pennsylvania could not flourish without taxes on all her land, even that owned by William Penn's descendants in England.

Franklin set off with his son as his only companion. His wife and his daughter would not come, for they were afraid of the dangers of the sea. But he loved the sea and was never idle, even on shipboard. He studied the Gulf Stream, the whales, and the birds. Sometimes, when the ship was lying becalmed, he scared his fellow travelers by jumping overboard for a swim around the vessel. One day he noticed that the sea became calm when the cook threw a pail of oily water over the rail. Nothing escaped Benjamin Franklin. When he arrived in England, the English thought the best was not too good for the famous Dr. Franklin. They flattered him and they feasted him, and lords and common people alike listened to his wisdom and wit. This meant a great deal at a time when the English were likely to treat all

By Diligence and Patience,

the Mouse Ate in Two the Cable

Americans as younger brothers with no rights and little sense. Even the King's ministers lent an ear to his pleas. It was not easy to get yes for an answer, but Franklin was patient. Constantly he presented Pennsylvania's problems, and acted as unofficial ambassador for all the colonies. It was more than five years before he sailed home.

His townspeople crowded around him to hear of his serious talks and to laugh at his funny adventures abroad. He told how one day he was strolling around a little pond with a group of important men. One of them began to regret that the days of miracles were past. Franklin said he could perform a miracle. He would still the waves of the pond! Turning his back to the group, he went to the water's edge and waved his walking stick like a wand over the rippling waves. Lo and behold! In a moment the water became as smooth as a mirror. Franklin laughed to himself. He had filled his hollow walking stick with oil and had sprinkled it over the water. Franklin never missed a trick. He had learned this one from the cook on shipboard.

But soon no American felt like laughing any longer. Anger and resentment against the mother country were growing among the colonists. England wanted their money but refused to grant them the full rights of citizens. She put higher and higher taxes upon them.

Men and Melons

Are Hard to Know

Many Americans grumbled. They said that they had come to the New World to be free and not to be bondsmen of England. They wanted to throw off all ties and be independent. But others said that the English were their brothers and that their quarrel could be mended. If the right Americans could talk to the King, he would see their side of things. Again Dr. Franklin was asked to go to England.

For ten long years Franklin stayed in England. He was sick and unhappy, and he was growing old. His faithful wife died in Philadelphia, and his son left him to side with the English. Franklin tried to keep peace. But the hotheads on both sides of the Atlantic wanted no peacemaker. The Americans thought he was too slow, the English thought he was too sly. He was called before the Privy Council, where the angry lords abused and humiliated him in public. Benjamin Franklin finally saw that peace was not possible. If he did not want to be thrown into jail, he must sail home at once.

When at last he reached home, the fighting had started. The hour had come for the American colonies to join together and throw off the English rule. In Independence Hall in Philadelphia, Franklin and men chosen from all the colonies gathered for the Second Continental Congress. Brilliant young Thomas Jefferson wrote the

No Gains

Without Pains

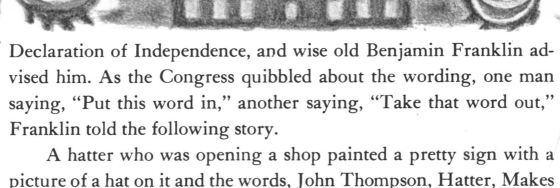

Declaration of Independence, and wise old Benjamin Franklin advised him. As the Congress quibbled about the wording, one man saying, "Put this word in," another saying, "Take that word out," Franklin told the following story.

A hatter who was opening a shop painted a pretty sign with a picture of a hat on it and the words, John Thompson, Hatter, Makes and Sells Hats for Ready Money. Before he hung his sign, he proudly showed it to his friends. The first one thought he should take out the word "Hatter," for the sign said "Makes Hats." It was painted out. The second said, "Take out the 'Makes,' for if people liked the hats they would not care who had made them." "Makes" was painted out. The third said, "Why 'Ready Money'? People who buy expect to pay." It was painted out. The fourth said, "Why 'Sells'? Nobody expects you to give your hats away." The last friend said, "Why 'Hats'? There is a picture of a hat on the sign." At last nothing was left but the name, John Thompson, and the picture of a hat.

At last on July 4, 1776, the Declaration, which proclaimed to the world that the thirteen American colonies were united as a free and independent country, was approved. As he signed his name, Franklin looked around him and said to the other signers: "We must indeed all hang together, or most assuredly we shall all hang separately."

Rebellion to Tyrants

Is Obedience to God

The thirteen colonies promised one another to hang together, whatever happened. But even unity wasn't enough to win a war of independence. They had to have soldiers and weapons and they needed money to fight the war.

George Washington was made Commander in Chief and began to train his troops. The army was in good hands. Franklin was asked to go to France to try to get help. The French were friendly toward the rebellious Americans, for England and France were enemies then. And of all Americans, Benjamin Franklin was the nearest to the heart of the French. They loved his inventions and his wit. The sayings of Poor Richard were almost as famous in France as at home. To them he was the wizard from the vast American wilderness.

So once again Dr. Franklin, who was now an old man of seventy, set off on the perilous journey. Two grandsons went along to keep him company, and he took in his luggage everything that was dear to his heart, from his smallest printing press to a bathtub he had had made for himself. He was too old to jump overboard for his swim; so he softened his aching joints in hot water in his tub. In order not to waste time while he lay in his bath, he had covered the tub with a lid where visitors could sit and chat with him. Only his head stuck

A Lie Stands On One Leg, Truth on Two

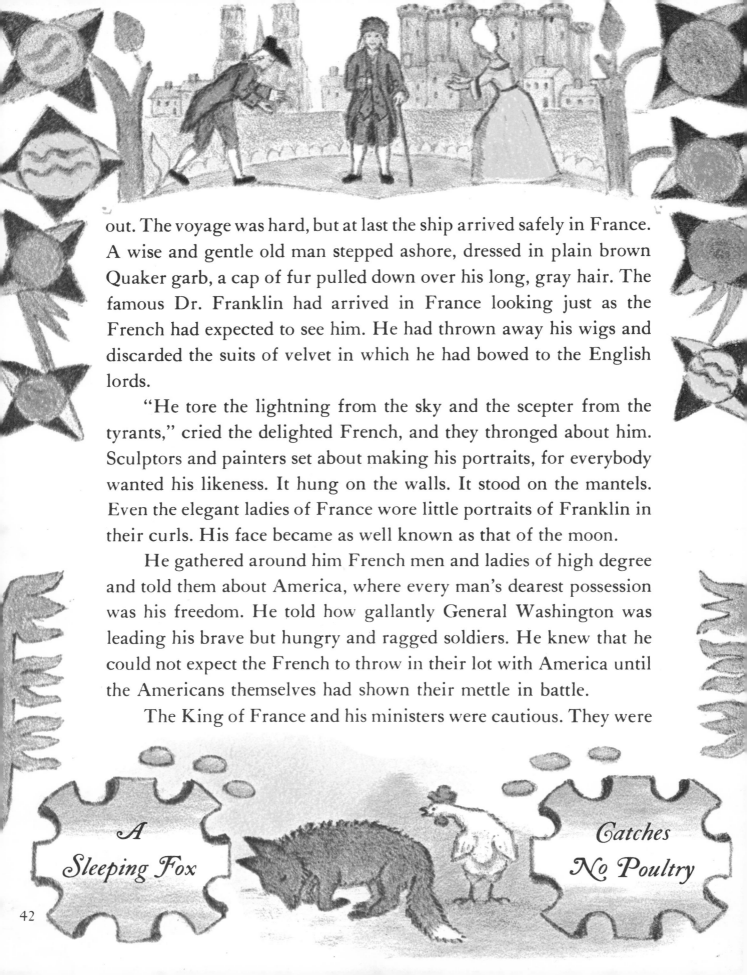

out. The voyage was hard, but at last the ship arrived safely in France. A wise and gentle old man stepped ashore, dressed in plain brown Quaker garb, a cap of fur pulled down over his long, gray hair. The famous Dr. Franklin had arrived in France looking just as the French had expected to see him. He had thrown away his wigs and discarded the suits of velvet in which he had bowed to the English lords.

"He tore the lightning from the sky and the scepter from the tyrants," cried the delighted French, and they thronged about him. Sculptors and painters set about making his portraits, for everybody wanted his likeness. It hung on the walls. It stood on the mantels. Even the elegant ladies of France wore little portraits of Franklin in their curls. His face became as well known as that of the moon.

He gathered around him French men and ladies of high degree and told them about America, where every man's dearest possession was his freedom. He told how gallantly General Washington was leading his brave but hungry and ragged soldiers. He knew that he could not expect the French to throw in their lot with America until the Americans themselves had shown their mettle in battle.

The King of France and his ministers were cautious. They were

A Sleeping Fox

Catches No Poultry

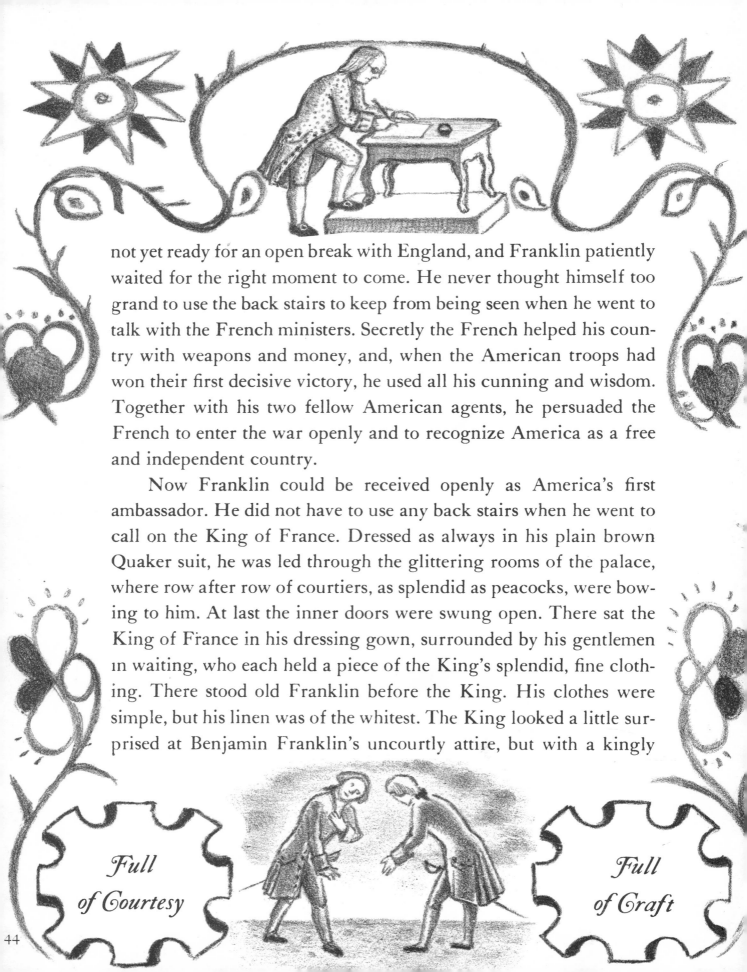

not yet ready for an open break with England, and Franklin patiently waited for the right moment to come. He never thought himself too grand to use the back stairs to keep from being seen when he went to talk with the French ministers. Secretly the French helped his country with weapons and money, and, when the American troops had won their first decisive victory, he used all his cunning and wisdom. Together with his two fellow American agents, he persuaded the French to enter the war openly and to recognize America as a free and independent country.

Now Franklin could be received openly as America's first ambassador. He did not have to use any back stairs when he went to call on the King of France. Dressed as always in his plain brown Quaker suit, he was led through the glittering rooms of the palace, where row after row of courtiers, as splendid as peacocks, were bowing to him. At last the inner doors were swung open. There sat the King of France in his dressing gown, surrounded by his gentlemen in waiting, who each held a piece of the King's splendid, fine clothing. There stood old Franklin before the King. His clothes were simple, but his linen was of the whitest. The King looked a little surprised at Benjamin Franklin's uncourtly attire, but with a kingly

Full of Courtesy

Full of Craft

44

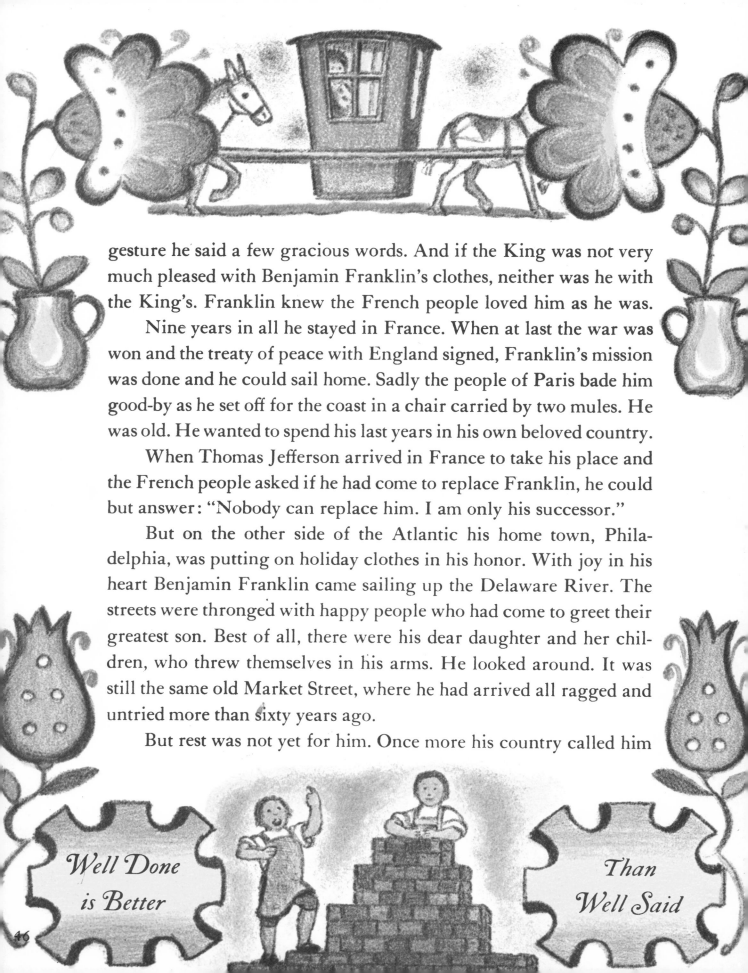

gesture he said a few gracious words. And if the King was not very much pleased with Benjamin Franklin's clothes, neither was he with the King's. Franklin knew the French people loved him as he was.

Nine years in all he stayed in France. When at last the war was won and the treaty of peace with England signed, Franklin's mission was done and he could sail home. Sadly the people of Paris bade him good-by as he set off for the coast in a chair carried by two mules. He was old. He wanted to spend his last years in his own beloved country.

When Thomas Jefferson arrived in France to take his place and the French people asked if he had come to replace Franklin, he could but answer: "Nobody can replace him. I am only his successor."

But on the other side of the Atlantic his home town, Philadelphia, was putting on holiday clothes in his honor. With joy in his heart Benjamin Franklin came sailing up the Delaware River. The streets were thronged with happy people who had come to greet their greatest son. Best of all, there were his dear daughter and her children, who threw themselves in his arms. He looked around. It was still the same old Market Street, where he had arrived all ragged and untried more than sixty years ago.

But rest was not yet for him. Once more his country called him

Well Done is Better

Than Well Said

to work. The newborn United States was free of England, new laws had to be made. Benjamin Franklin was one of the men who drew up and signed the Constitution. His spirit rings through the glorious words that "secure the blessings of liberty to ourselves and our posterity."

Old Benjamin Franklin looked about him and beheld his wonderful country, wide and free, and he pointed to the emblem of the sun in Independence Hall. He had never quite known what it meant.

"Now I know," he said, "that it is a rising sun."

Then at last he was ready to rest. He sat in his garden in the shade of a mulberry tree and watched his grandchildren play around him. He retired to the quiet of his library, where now he could read his beloved books in peace.

And when his hour came, Benjamin Franklin said: "I am ready to repose myself securely in the lap of God and Nature, as a child in the arms of an affectionate parent."

Content is the Philosopher' Stone,

that Turns All it Touches into Gold

THIEVES' WORLD

GRAPHICS 1

Adapted and Scripted
By Robert Lynn Asprin and Lynn Abbey

Artwork by Tim Sale   Edited by Laurie Sutton
Publisher Liaison—Kay Reynolds

Starblaze Graphics—The Donning Company/Publishers
Norfolk/Virginia Beach • 1985

Thieves' World Graphics 1 is the first book of a continuing series of graphic novels based on the **Thieves' World** anthologies published by Ace Books and contributed to by:

Lynn Abbey
Poul Anderson
Robert Lynn Asprin
Robin Bailey
John Brunner
C. J. Cherryh
Christine DeWees
David Drake

Diane Duane
Philip Jose Farmer
Joe Haldeman
Vonda McIntyre
Chris & Janet Morris
Andrew J. Offutt
Diana Paxson
A. E. Van Vogt

Look for further volumes of **Thieves' World Graphics** to be published quarterly. This is only one of many graphic novels and series published by The Donning Company/Publishers. For a complete listing of our titles, please write to the address below.

The Donning Company/Publishers
5659 Virginia Beach Boulevard
Norfolk, Virginia 23502

10 9 8 7 6 5 4 3 2 1

Library of Congress Cataloging-in-Publication Data

Asprin, Robert.
  Thieves' world graphics #1
  Adapted from the Thieves' World anthologies.
  I. Abbey, Lynn. II. Sale, Tim. III. Sutton, Laurie. IV. Title. V. Title: Thieves' world no. 1. VI. Title: Thieves' world number one.
PS3551.S6T5   1985   813'.54   85-16297
ISBN 0-89865-415-7 (pbk.)

Printed in the United States of America

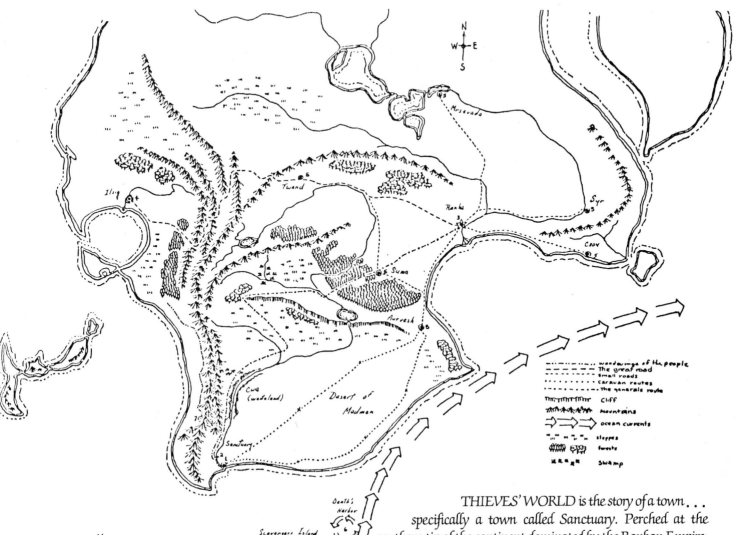

the immediate continent

THIEVES' WORLD is the story of a town . . . specifically a town called Sanctuary. Perched at the southern tip of the continent dominated by the Rankan Empire, Sanctuary was founded by slaves from the city of Ilsig who took advantage of a war between Ilsig and Ranke to escape and flee south. Their freedom was cut short, however, as Sanctuary itself was conquered by the Empire and used as a caravan stop between Ranke and the now-defeated satellite city of Ilsig.

Sanctuary prospered until Ranke succeeded in putting down the last stronghold of resistance and opened up a shorter, northern mountain route between the two cities. Now forgotten and unwanted, Sanctuary has fallen on hard times. Those who were able have moved on to more profitable cities, leaving the town to the desperate and petty criminals who have come to use it as a refuge . . . people more concerned with survival than morals.

As our chronicles open, the Rankan Emperor has decided to remove his step-brother, Prince Kadakithis, as a potential rival for the throne by having him posted as the new military governor of Sanctuary. In his youthful idealism, the prince takes the assignment seriously and plans to clean up the crime and corruption which currently abound in the city, a plan which the citizens of Sanctuary greet with mixed enthusiasm. . . .

SOMEONE IS ALWAYS AWAKE IN SANCTUARY...

...ESPECIALLY WHEN OTHERS ARE SLEEPING!

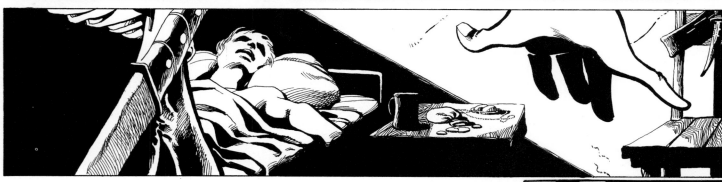

MMM— WHO? SHADOWSPAWN!

HUSH..! I HAVE A PRESENT FOR YOU.

MORNING...

GLAD SHE DIDN'T *WAKE UP...* DIDN'T WANT HER READING TOO MUCH INTO THE VISIT.

HOPE SHE REMEMBERS NOT TO WEAR THAT DAMN NECKLACE IN PUBLIC...

"THERE ARE THIEVES IN THIS TOWN...

...AND EVEN *HONEST* MEN HAVE AN EYE FOR EASY PROFIT! "

... SO THERE HE WAS, CONFRONTED BY A CREATURE OF MAGIC ...

A CREATURE AS LARGE AS...

...A HOUSE!

PERHAPS THE YOUNG GENTLEMAN WOULD LIKE TO TELL THE TALE WHILE HAKIEM LISTENS.

I PAID FOR THIS STORY! SHUT UP AND LET HAKIEM TELL IT!

ONE SIDE OLD MAN!!

ZALBAR!

THERE'S NO NEED TO BE RUDE.

I HOPE WE DIDN'T DISTURB YOUR STORY. HERE... PERHAPS THIS WILL MAKE UP FOR OUR INTRUSION.

ONE GOLD COIN SEEMS SMALL PAYMENT FOR SCARING THESE PRECIOUS CHILDREN...

THOSE *GUTTERSNIPES*? A GOLD COIN COULD BUY THE LOT OF THEM...

...AND THEIR SISTERS!

THAT'S ENOUGH...

BUT YOUR HIGHNESS, THIS MAN IS ONLY PLAYING ON YOUR...

CAPTAIN...

BUT YOUR...

CAPTAIN...

IF HE IS, IT'S MY MONEY TO GIVE.

BUT...!

NOW COME ALONG.

I WISH TO SEE THE BAZAAR.

IS THAT THE NEW GOVERNOR? THE PRINCE?

MY BROTHER SAYS THE EMPEROR SENT HIM HERE TO GET HIM OUT OF THE CAPITAL!

HE AND HIS *HELL HOUNDS* WILL CHANGE EVERYTHING!

WON'T THEY, HAKIEM?

HAKIEM?

MOST COMINGS AND GOINGS IN SANCTUARY GO UNNOTICED...

...SOME ARE NOT.

THAT'S AYE-GOPHLAN... THE GARRISON CAPTAIN.

WHAT'S HE DOING IN THIS PART OF TOWN?

HE'S HEADED FOR MY MASTERS' SHOP.

IF MELILOT THINKS I'VE BROUGHT HIM, MAYBE I'LL GET THE ASSIGNMENT... OR AT LEAST GET A TIP!

MAY I TAKE A MESSAGE *DIRECTLY* TO MY MASTER, CAPTAIN?

AH! I HAVE ... **NEED** OF A DISCREET TRANSLATOR. IF YOU WOULD ANNOUNCE ME?

THE CAPTAINS' BUSINESS BETTER BE IMPORTANT... I INTERRUPTED MELILOT'S LUNCH FOR IT.

JARVEENA! COME IN HERE!

GODS BELOW! MASTER MELILOT'S LET HIS LUNCH GO COLD!

YOUR APPRENTICE CAN SOLVE THIS MYSTERY?

I SUSPECT YOUR SCROLL WAS WRITTEN IN YENIZED.

JARVEENA WAS BORN THERE. SHE'LL RECOGNIZE THE SCRIPT, AND BE ABLE TO READ IT AS WELL.

WON'T YOU, MY LITTLE ONE?

SUSPECT?! MY MASTER CAN RECOGNIZE ANY LANGUAGE... AND HE'S NEVER CALLED ME HIS LITTLE ONE.

NOW HE'S SIGNALLING TO ME. MELILOT MUST HAVE SOME SCHEME IN MIND...

...BETTER PLAY ALONG WITH IT.

WHAT'S THIS?!

THE WRITING MOVES! IT'S ALIVE!

THE WORDS REACH RIGHT INTO MY MIND!

GOT TO FIGHT IT... LOOK AWAY!

I BELIEVE THIS IS YENIZED, AS YOU SAID, SIR.

BELIEVE ?! CAN'T YOU READ IT ?

I KNOW COMMON YENIZED, SIR. THIS IS HIGH YENIZEN, FOR POETS AND PRINCES.

WE'LL NEED A FEW DAYS TO TRANSLATE IT... THAT'S ALL.

WAIT HERE WHILE I SEE THE CAPTAIN OUT.

YOU'RE A SMART LITTLE WEASEL.

CAN YOU GUESS WHAT'S ON THAT SCROLL?

MAGIC..?

SO ONLY THE RIGHT PERSON READS IT?

UMM... OUR CAPTAIN SAYS HE FOUND IT ON THE PARADE GROUND, DROPPED BY THE RANKAN COMMANDER THAT ESCORTED THE PRINCE INTO TOWN.

HE SEEMS TO THINK THERE'S MORE TO BE GAINED BY READING IT THAN RETURNING IT.

OF COURSE, THE CAPTAIN CAN'T READ HIS OWN NAME.

BUT WHAT... WHY BRING IT HERE?

AH... I AM A FOOL. HE DOESN'T *SEE* THE MAGIC!

VERY GOOD. HAVE SOME LOBSTER.

YOU'LL NEED YOUR STRENGTH FOR YOUR ERRAND TONIGHT.

ERRAND?

I WANT YOU TO ASK COMMANDER NIZHARU WHICH IS WORTH MORE: THE RETURN OF HIS SCROLL...

..OR THE *HEAD OF* AYE-GOPHLAN.

"SEEK HIM AFTER CURFEW IN THE TENTS OUTSIDE THE PALACE."

YOU FIVE MEN HAVE BEEN SELECTED TO STAY WITH ME AFTER NIZHARU AND THE OTHERS LEAVE TOMORROW AFTERNOON.

IT'S BEEN A LONG TIME, *HANSE*. YOU USUALLY GO TO *MOONFLOWER* WITH YOUR QUESTIONS.

SHE ISN'T AROUND TODAY... MY PROBLEM WON'T WAIT.

AND IT'S *SHADOWSPAWN* NOT *HANSE*.

YOU CHOOSE YOUR NAME AS YOU CHOSE YOUR LIFE.

BUT YOU DIDN'T COME TO CHAT. YOU HAVE A PROBLEM?

YES. I CAN'T TELL YOU EXACTLY, BUT...

NEVER MIND. THAT'S FOR RICH CUSTOMERS, NOT OLD FRIENDS.

DIVIDE THE CARDS INTO THREE PILES WHILE THINKING ABOUT YOUR PROBLEM...

YOU DON'T NEED TO TELL ME! I REMEMBER.

THERE.

TRY YOUR S'DANZO SIGHT ON THAT.

Archway

Zigzurrat

HALF-S'DANZO.

NOW BE QUIET AND LET ME CONCENTRATE.

THE ARCHWAY... RIGHT OF PASSAGE... THERE WILL BE A MAJOR CHANGE IN YOUR PERSONAL LIFE.

THE ZIGZURRAT... CATACLYSMIC CHANGE... THE CHANGE WILL AFFECT YOU EXTERNALLY AS WELL AS INTERNALLY... POSSIBLY SOMETHING TO DO WITH A LARGE STONE BUILDING... I'M NOT SURE...

THE UNENDING CIRCLE... THE CONSTANCY OF JEWELS OR JEWELRY ITSELF... THE MORE THINGS CHANGE, THE MORE THEY STAY THE SAME...

EXCUSE ME, COMMANDER NIZHARU.

WHAT!?

WHO ARE YOU BOY?

HOW DID YOU GET HERE?

BY THE GODS...! IT'S *HIM!* IF HE REMEMBERS!

NO, HE CALLED ME 'BOY'. HE DOESN'T RECOGNIZE ME ... YET.

'IT WAS SHOWN TO ME BY A CAPTAIN OF THE GUARDS. MY MASTER THINKS THE CAPTAIN COULD NOT HAVE OBTAINED IT HONESTLY...

'FOR SURELY AN *IMPERIAL COMMANDER* WOULD NOT HAVE DROPPED IT ON THE PARADE GROUND.'

MY MASTER, MELILOT THE SCRIPTOR, HAS LEARNED OF A SCROLL HE THINKS BELONGS TO YOU.

NEVER.

IT IS MY MASTERS' THOUGHT THAT WE MAY BE OF SERVICE TO YOU — THAT WE MIGHT PROVIDE A FALSE READING OF THE SCROLL.

FOR SURELY THE *CAPTAIN* IS THE *LEAST* OF THOSE WHO CONSPIRE AGAINST YOU...

...AND IT IS THEIR *MASTERS* YOU NEED, AS MUCH AS THE SCROLL.

MADAME?

TAKE THE YOUNG MAN TO CEYLENE... THE LAVENDER ROOM, I THINK.

CHILDREN,,,!

"...STILL, IT HELPS PAY FOR THE NEW GUARDS."

THE APHRODISIA HOUSE?

WHY NOT? IT'S THE RICHEST HOUSE ON THE STREET.

I WOULDN'T KNOW. I'VE NEVER BEEN IN IT.

DAMN! ALL THE ROOMS ARE BUSY.

WE'LL HAVE TO TRY SOMEWHERE ELSE.

WE'RE *ALREADY* HERE! THERE'S NOTHING TO SAY IT WILL BE BETTER ELSEWHERE.

HERE, LET ME TRY.

STILL THINK I'M TOO CAUTIOUS, EH?

ALL RIGHT, WE'LL TRY IT YOUR WAY.

OH, YES... YES!

WHAT'S TAKING SO LONG?

I... I CAN'T QUITE REACH.

CUDGET?

A BRIBE OR A HAND.

IT'S THE RISKS OF THE GAME IN SANCTUARY.

THE NEXT MORNING...

HE WAS KIND — AS WELL AS SKILLED. HE SAW... KNEW ALL OF ME.

AND HE LOVED ME...

...NO WONDER THE OTHER MAGES CURSED HIM.

I DON'T... OH! HE RETURNED ME TO MY ROOM.

NICE.

HE WAS PRETTY NICE HIMSE... WHAT?

SCALES!?!

SO THERE YOU ARE, YOU LITTLE SLUT!

KILLED *WHO?*

A *BLIND*... AN INFORMER WHO WAS *NOT* AN INFORMER. IT WAS DONE TO PROVIDE AN EXAMPLE... AS YOU ORDERED.

YES, YES. GO ON.

THERE IS CONSTERNATION ON THE AVENUE OF TEMPLES OVER THE NEW SHRINES TO...

DOES IT AFFECT OUR OPERATIONS?

NO, BUT I THOUGHT YOU'D LIKE TO KNOW...

NOW I KNOW. NEXT ITEM.

... TWO OF YOUR HAWKMASKS WERE REFUSED SERVICE AT THE VULGAR UNICORN LAST NIGHT BY ONE-THUMB...

I KNOW ONE-THUMB. IF HE REFUSED THEM SERVICE, IT WAS BECAUSE OF THEIR OWN ACTIONS, NOT BECAUSE OF ANY ILL FEELINGS TOWARD ME.

NEXT ITEM.

... WE MAY HAVE TO CUT BACK ON OUR OVERT OPERATIONS BECAUSE OF THE NEW HELL-HOUNDS IN TOWN...

WHY?

THE HELL HOUNDS ARE GOOD, JUBAL. YOUR HAWKMASKS ARE AFRAID...

MY MEN? AFRAID OF GUARDSMEN? I THOUGHT I WAS PAYING GOOD GOLD TO HAVE THE FINEST SWORDS IN SANCTUARY AT MY DISPOSAL?

THE HELL HOUNDS AREN'T *FROM* SANCTUARY! BEFORE THEY ARRIVED I WOULD HAVE SAID OURS WERE THE BEST SWORDS. NOW...

THE HELL HOUNDS! IT SEEMS ALL ANY-ONE CAN *TALK* ABOUT IS THE HELL HOUNDS!

AND YOU SHOULD LISTEN!

FORGIVE ME, JUBAL, BUT YOU KNOW YOUR MEN ARE NOT *COWARDS* OR *CHILDREN* WHEN IT COMES TO BATTLE. WHEN THEY TRY TO WARN YOU ABOUT A NEW FORCE IN TOWN, YOU SHOULD *LISTEN*, NOT MOCK THEM!

VERY WELL, SALIMAN.

TELL ME ABOUT THE HELL HOUNDS.

THEY WERE HANDPICKED FROM THE ROYAL ELITE GUARD ESPECIALLY FOR THIS ASSIGNMENT... CHOSEN FOR THEIR SKILL AT ARMS...

...AND THEIR *UNSWERVING* LOYALTY.

SINCE THEIR ARRIVAL IN SANCTUARY, EVERY EFFORT TO BRIBE OR ASSASSINATE THEM HAS ENDED IN *DEATH* FOR WHOEVER ATTEMPTED IT.

I SEE YOUR POINT.

STILL, THEY ARE MEN... AND MEN HAVE WEAK- NESSES. TELL OUR INFORMANTS—

WHAT?

WE CAUGHT THIS GUTTER-RAT ON THE GROUNDS... PROBABLY TRYING TO *STEAL* SOME- THING.

IF I WAS GOING TO STEAL, YOU WOULDN'T HAVE CAUGHT ME! LET GO!

JUSTICE IN SANCTUARY, WHEN IT *OCCURS*, IS SWIFT.

NIZHARU DANCES AT THE END OF A ROPE BEFORE THE HOUR IS OUT.

JARVEENA WATCHES FROM THE SHADOW OF THE PALACE WALLS.

HE RUNS AWAY FROM THE PRINCE... AND IT'S OVER! THEY DON'T *NEED* MY OATHS AND STORY!

I COULDN'T EVEN WRITE THE EXECUTION ORDER—

IMPERIAL TREASON DOESN'T NEED ONE!

YOU HIDE YOUR EMOTIONS WELL.

ENAS YORL?

THE SAME.

INASMUCH AS I CAN EVER MAKE THE STATEMENT.

ARE YOU CONTENT?

IT WAS THE *PRINCE'S* VENGEANCE, NOT MINE.

TO SPEAK AFTER PRINCES IS A DANGEROUS HABIT. SECOND-HAND REVENGE MAY NOT BE AS *SWEET*... BUT IT'S SAFE.

I LIVED FOR ONE THING ONLY — AND NOW IT'S GONE. I DIDN'T *PAY* FOR SAFETY.

REMEMBER WHAT I TOLD YOU ABOUT SPELLS: THEY SEEK THEIR OWN PATHS. YOU PAID A FAIR PRICE TO BIND NIZHARU'S DEATH TO THAT SCROLL...

...BUT NOT ENOUGH FOR VENGEANCE.

HAVEN'T YOU FORGOTTEN WHAT ELSE WAS ON THAT SCROLL?

THE SECOND DEATH?

THAT SCROLL WAS SEALED IN RANKE.

ITS SPELLS WERE CAST BY HAZARD MAGES WORTHY OF THEIR DEGREES. I COULD CHANGE THE COURSE OF THE STREAM...

...BUT I COULD NEVER STOP ITS FLOW.

THE SCROLL IS LEGIBLE; NIZHARU IS DEAD...

AND ANOTHER DEATH MUST OCCUR!

WHOSE DEATH?

MINE?

IT COULD BE THAT ANY DEATH WILL SATISFY THE ORIGINAL SPELL CASTING—

BUT PERHAPS NOT.

IT WOULD BE SAFEST TO LEAVE THIS PLACE. EVEN WITHOUT THE SPELLS, SANCTUARY IS NO PLACE TO REBUILD YOUR LIFE.

NOT EVEN VENGEANCE COULD REBUILD MY LIFE.

NOW,,, I'LL SHOW YOU THE SECRETS OF THE APHRODISIA HOUSE.

I THINK I'VE ALREADY FOUND THEM.

THERE ARE MORE.

COME.

APPARENTLY YOUR PRINCE THINKS THAT THE STREET WAS BUILT OUTSIDE THE WALLS BECAUSE THE FOUNDING FATHERS OF SANCTUARY DISAPPROVED OF US.

IN REALITY, WE ARE NOT OUTSIDE THE WALLS AT ALL.

LOOK AROUND YOU... AS A MILITARY MAN. OUR WALLS ARE FOUR FEET THICK...

... THE SHUTTERS OF THE HARDEST WOOD FROM THE MOUNTAINS...

... OUR HOUSES ARE PART OF THE WALL...

... AND BELOW...

...WE HAVE OUR OWN WELLS AND STOREROOMS THAT COULD SUPPLY THE CITY FOR WEEKS IF NECESSARY.

YOU COULD HIDE THE ENTIRE GARRISON DOWN HERE ... WITH TUNNELS THAT LEAD FROM HERE TO THE SWAMP OF NIGHT SECRETS, OR INTO SANCTUARY, OR EVEN INTO THE GOVERNORS PALACE!

WE ARE A PART OF THE CITY'S DEFENSE. WHOEVER HAS RULED IN SANCTUARY HAS ALWAYS SOUGHT OUR COOPERATION.

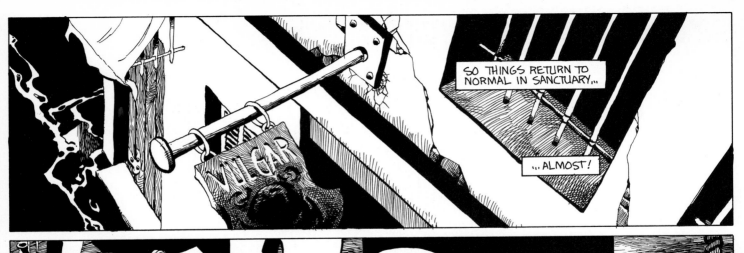

End

Afterword

You'd think it would be easy to create a graphic novel adaptation of a best-selling anthology series. The characters and the stories are already set up so all you have to do is add art. Easy.

IT ISN'T!!

After completing this first issue of **Thieves' World Graphics 1**, I have a new respect for those who try to adapt popular fantasy works like *Conan* or **The Lord of the Rings** into illustrated adaptations or movies. Everything visual has to be scratch-built from costumes to hair styles to interiors and exteriors. You have to determine how each and every character is supposed to look. What's more, no matter how carefully you work, the end result invariably differs from what the readers envisioned.

With **Thieves' World Graphics,** we were faced with several additional problems...or rather, a new incarnation of an old problem. **Thieves' World** has always broken new ground and this graphic novel version of the story is no exception. Specifically, everyone involved in the project wanted it to be something new, a change of pace from the usual "good guy(s) punch out/kill/blow up bad guy(s)" fare which predominates the comic field today. We wanted **Thieves' World** to look like a graphic novel series, not a throwaway item with a superficial story line meant solely for the children's market, but something adults would enjoy as well. Something they would want to read and collect. Consequently, this project is in many ways a grand experiment: the stories are less action oriented, the characters are more intricate than is currently deemed "saleable" in today's comic/graphic market. In many ways, we're taking quite a chance in going beyond formula formats, but we feel that you—the literate audience we want to reach—are worth the gamble. If you like the illustrated book format, the comic format, what do you really have to read nowadays once you've outgrown the standard superhero book? There isn't much on hand. We hope **Thieves' World Graphics** will provide you with an alternative form of entertainment.

Fortunately, there have been some exceptionally fine people working on the project with us. While there is information on them in the Bio portion of this publication, I feel they are due special plaudits in this afterwords.

Tim Sale has handled all the artwork from layouts through pencils to inking. While the quality of his work speaks for itself, it is all the more incredible when you realize that before this book, the longest solo graphic project he had undertaken was only five pages long.

Lynn Abbey, my wife and co-editor/manager of the **Thieves' World** empire, went from a standing start of zero comics background (she had never even read them) to put herself through a crash course in the field to provide invaluable input and advice on backgrounds and scripting in this first issue.

Laurie Sutton provided desperately needed expertise in the graphics field to guide and coordinate the efforts of totally inexperienced scriptors and artist in these crucial early stages of development.

The staff and management of Donning/Starblaze have been unswerving in their support of this project from its conception. One hears so many horror stories of creator/publisher brawls that it's a pleasure to report our publisher has not once failed to provide the financing, promotion, conferences, information, enthusiasm, respect or concern for product quality that is so necessary to launch a project of this nature.

The result of all our best efforts is now in the hands of the final jury . . . you, the reader. This is the first of a series of quarterly publications that will continue until we either run out of material or the sales fail to make the publication economically practical. If you find the book disappointing, it will not be because we were unable to capture our vision on paper, but rather that our vision does not live up to your expectations. If, on the other hand, you find you are as pleased with our work as we are, drop a note off to the publisher . . . or, better still, buy another copy and give it to a friend.

Robert Lynn Asprin
September 1985
Ann Arbor, Michigan

who's who in
THIEVES' WORLD
GRAPHICS 1

Robert Lynn Asprin and **Lynn Abbey** are perhaps the most successful husband/wife, writers/editors team in fantasy literature today. Their **Thieves' World** shared universe anthology series has sold over a million copies and is currently credited with having created a new literary format. Each of them spent more than a decade in the corporate world before turning to writing: Bob as a cost accountant for Xerox, Lynn as a systems analyst for several insurance companies including Metropolitan Life and AAA. In addition to editing and now scripting graphic novels, they are each recognized writers in their own right. Lynn has three novels to her credit: **Daughter of the Bright Moon, The Black Flame** and **The Guardians.** Bob has written six books in the popular *Myth Adventures* series, **Another Fine Myth, Myth Conceptions, Myth Directions, Hit or Myth, Myth-Ing Persons** and **Little Myth Marker** as well as **Cold Cash War, The Bug Wars, Tambu,** and **Mirror Friend, Mirror Foe** (with George Takei).

Tim Sale attended the School of Visual Arts in Manhattan while simultaneously taking John Buscema's workshop in comic illustration. A loyal resident of Seattle, Washington, he started the Grey Archer Press with his sister and works closely with Northern Lights, a coalition of Northwest fantasy artists. Currently, Tim splits his time between the **Thieves' World Graphics** and inking the *Myth Adventures* graphic adaptation of Asprin's *Myth* books. Perhaps the most physically active of the team, he enjoys bicycling and soccer in his spare time.

Laurie Sutton has worked as an editor for both DC Comics and Marvel/Epic Comics but her enthusiasm and experience extend beyond the world of the graphic novel and comic format. Her sense of visual storytelling combined with her literary expertise make her the perfect editorial guide for the transition of **Thieves' World**'s existing prose into its new, illustrated home. Based in Manhattan, she is currently doing free-lance editing and writing. Her other interests include film, interior design, football, the study of *anything* Japanese, and aviation.

Kay Reynolds, the editor-in-chief (or Head-Ed) of Donning/Starblaze, has the thankless task of coordinating the efforts of the **Thieves' World Graphics** team with the production and marketing schedule of her company. With her heart in fandom and her head in the business world (accounting), Reynolds created the Starblaze Graphics line of comic illustrated adventure when she inititated the publication of **ElfQuest Books 1, 2, 3,** and **4,** the color volumes, in 1981 for Donning. Her skillful marketing of **ElfQuest** to mainstream bookstores opened the doors for a wider public exposure and acceptance of stories in the graphic novel format.